Coal Dust:
A Collection of Poems
From a Young Mountaineer

by

Sarah Whiteside Slocum

Printed in the United States of America

First Printing, 2012

ISBN 978-1-105-56653-0

OaksAndOrchids.Tumblr.com

Lulu.com

For some:
A cold kiss on the
Forehead,
Spit, smudged with
Midnight dust.

Dedicated To:

Alexander Henry Slocum, Jr.

&

William Corbett

CIRCULAR HEAT

Cat bath — coarse tongue
ruffs soft fur.
Your hand in mine, walking
down the street
or my hand on an oven burner.
All fried nerves before breakfast.

ALBANY AT NIGHT

Railroad tracks cut the streets
past dormitories and nuclear
reactors, under labs
where rats have their brains
dissected daily. Sometimes
it's them you smell in elevators,
stale formaldehyde and pet food.
Students shuffle, hands
jammed in pockets and chins tucked
in useless efforts to avoid
numbing wind that cracks
skin and makes you bleed.
Between door and Mass Ave
exactly five trees devoid of green
— they gave up their fight long ago —
against streetlights and halogens.
Gum splotched on sidewalk:
black, inverse stars.

Gray sky dawns, more often than not,
beautiful in its mute oppression
while milk trucks rattle loudly
under windows I can't ever
get to close.

OFF BALANCE

Something doesn’t feel right.
Two trains on the tracks —
dark brown and heavy.
Look like coal trains
but they’re not filled with home.
At least I don’t have to walk through
slush to learn my equations.
A step is crumbling on the stairs
of the Longfellow. I saw it on my run.
77 flanked by black banners, too modern.
Symmetrical, but out of place.
No one died, why black?
Walking on, a single doorknob twisted
45 degrees right. So wrong.
Can’t something line up? Even
one of my boots is ripping,
thread splitting up the back.
Is this what a stroke feels like?

When victims close their eyes and
one arm drifts down?
They can't. They never
know the difference.

STEEL THE WALL

Today, nestled in under
little dome, gloved hands
clutching a tea mug. Somewhere
below, a girl laughing
but I can't see her. I don't want to.
Better to listen to the electric
drill and watch the workman
install the tv display. There's
something calming about
power tools. They connect things.
Tight and strong. They leave
a mark and aren't shy about it.
Maybe, the nice man will let me ramset
a single nail to the wall, behind
the tv. No one else would
ever see it, but I'd know it was there.

FORGET FLYING

36 feet of stone holds up
our purpose. DEVELOPMENT
OF SCIENCE. Tour groups spin below,
craning to read the lofty words.
One spills his coffee. Too fast,
too fast. That's the first lesson:
how to slow down, and when.
And the higher up you get,
the closer to your purpose,
the more metal surrounds you.
Green and fading but sharp.
Snarling or snapping back,
holding you here, hostage.
And don't try to fly.
You won't get out, you'll just
crash into the glass, like
the sparrow who, just yesterday,
was singing above SCIENCE.

CLAIMED

Remember: Messages of sharpie

Tracing spiral galaxies
where my fingertips
meet your skin.
Senseless circles, conflation
of heat and darkness.

I've never wanted so badly
to cut your skin
and pour myself in,
as much as you
can stand,
then more.

Escape velocity
seems so slow.
We're already flying

but we're running
out of oxygen.

I gasp and stutter but
you bring me back.
Devour me, please,
in your unique
myriad of ways.
Silk sapphires
burnt in emerald
ash, radiant
nonetheless.

I could spin like this forever,
ecstasy in aftermath.
Avalanche, run.
Joy in danger
and terror in flight.

DON'T LET GO

So tenuous
the last brown speckled leaf clings
to a lean and rough branch,
as if it will turn green again
if it can hang on long enough.
It doesn't realize it was
born to die.
Late afternoon sunlight twirls
among trees and parking meters
carried by wind, ebb or flow.
The bridge, red,
carrying US 1 north to Olson
on rusty legs.
51 degrees and no clouds,
not typical for December in Chelsea.
There's a woman pushing a
stroller with no baby inside
but packages instead,

dragging the toddler along in her wake
as he kicks up the ones that failed.

SALTED STEPS

It's time for class, so I go
out from the warmth of heaters into ice.
Every person is their own world,
bundled and breathing steam,
young dragons in winter. First,
down Albany a maintenance van
blocks the sidewalk, loud diesel
chugs or purring. Then, onto Mass Ave,
where morning runners dodge
snow and puddles,
trying to outrun the cold.
And each other, I guess.
I look at my reflection in passing glass
but all I see are eyes and wool.
                                        On
to 77, where WILLIAM BARTON ROGERS
welcomes me with stone columns and
(thankfully) salted steps. Inside,

everyone strips three layers,
like deer shedding antlers.
There's nothing new here, just
8:30 on a Tuesday.

BROKEN

It's 3:20 but it's not. It's
actually 4:34
so at 3:20 4:35 I go to
Porter Square to get my watch fixed
it's no longer October 15
It's always funny that there's one
person who stands on the left of an
escalator even when signs say STAND
ON RIGHT and the people look like a
line of ants but I take the stairs
got to keep your heart healthy and
all that
And there's the normal people women
pushing strollers men in business suits
a woman with a shopping cart entirely
filled with zucchini must be 40 pounds
and an iPod
And I write this all in gold sitting next to

some Harvard grad spewing politics and
grasping their purse like it holds the
nuclear launch codes or a snickers bar

Those damned anime faces.

And then I go to starbucks and I get
a latte please yellow #5 tartrazine
next door four sunflowers for a friend
who isn't feeling so good
write in paint when you can't find a pen
two pages now cuz paint ain't a ten
point font more like the side of
a building in Marigold with prayer
flags and giant envelopes

5:59 and right it's only two stops but
it's a trip and maybe
I'll mail this one to Frank

T

I'm going to the movies, so I
walk down Mass Ave towards
Central Square headed for the
red line to green line to AMC.
As O'Hara would say it's
20 till 8 on a Wednesday night
but he isn't here anymore.
I pass the gay clubs and
swanky dinner joints
where men in ties pull out chairs
to seat their "ladies".
I would fall down, I think
trip over some hemline or
old Coca—Cola can.
Glass bottle, really, since
that's how they used to come
in six packs with a red carrier.

I hear a train through the grates
lining the sidewalk like mini canyons
and I run, dodging the homeless yelping
for spare change and the three-legged dog
that eats more than I do.
I squeeze on the train and
look around at the
ORIGINAL VOICEMAIL ads and I blush.
They're corny but cute too.

I emerge next to the emerald necklace,
but now its not so emerald,
more like ruby
and fire or sunlight.
George Winston drifts out of a book store.
It's *DECEMBER* but it's not.
Chicago comes on and that's better
for now since there's a park nearby
but it's not Saturday
and I'm five minutes late

but he’s still waiting outside to
get the door for me.

NIGHTLIGHTS

First trip to strip club
Hour and a half talking to a dancer
—what why when where
and *how much*?—
Americans and eastern europeans
Blonde brunette and star tattoos
shriek when they slide down pole
Sounds painful to me
but I'd still like to try sometime

You can have just as much fun
sitting in the corner and
watching the bachelor's party
drink Bud and throw singles
at the blonde upside-down on stage
Mesmerized by cheap, house wine
and purplish-blue lights where
her lower abs meet upper thigh

IDES OF OCTOBER

Cat in sun spot
— all dark fur and
white lines

L

There was a scratch
on the silver frame,
so you took it and
scratched it more.
“There,” you said.
That settled it.
Could you, please,
come back and settle me?

HOOD RIVER

Contrast between red stop sign
and blue sky. Hard to tell where one ends
and other begins. Columbia River Gorge
stretching wide her rock arms.

Park the rental on a slope,
head into Dog River Coffee.
Chai latte for me, and you had
a dark roast. "Drip," you said.

Pass art galleries
and the Double Mountain brewery.
Craft beer.

And then I see it.
The sign at the farmer's market
while you bought two peaches.
SATURDAY DOG WASH.

Yes, this is it. I'm meant
to live here.

Young man with a gorgeous boxer.
Golden retriever shaking off
soap suds, drying in the August
late-morning sun.
More dogs than I could ever pet.

Sadly, back to car. Got to
cross Mount Hood before dark.
Marathon tomorrow in Deschutes.

A Texan's note on the windshield –
"Sorry 'bout the bumper. I'm not used
to driving on hills."
Hills? Right. This might be a 3% grade.
Onwards.

WE ARE…

Not even 0730 but
rain beats into gutters,
keeping me awake this Tuesday.
Only downside — strips my tree
of her bright red and yellow mantle,
she's shrinking daily.
Up, fog-entombed hill has
lights flashing to warn airplanes,
but we turned the fountain off
yesterday.

TU ME MANQUES

6:11 on a Sunday
view from road:
middle-aged man rests
forehead against stone
—μάρμαρον—
Who were you?

BIRD BY BIRD

Bird walks on ledge
backdrop of setting sun
between two small trees
I don’t know what kind they are
I've never been good at that
You can look into this sun,
brilliance broken by limbs and ramble
but still see ever-moving spots on paper

Bird shadow melds with that of tree,
brown stake among golden rays.
The air is getting chilly
just enough to bite, say thanks
for residual heat seeping upwards
from concrete curb and
asphalt parking lot
into my five-fingers and denim.

Birds emerge from shadow,
not one now but three.
Flap out over brush and double train
tracks where the crickets sing
and moms say goodnight.

SUMMER TRACKS

Evening sun turns green leaves gold
this next to last day of August.
Baby oaks guard the tracks,
swaying in time with *cha-chugs*,
monotone but melodic somehow.
Maybe it's all in my head
but I'd swear those hundred cars can sing.

ROCKY GAP

Fog dances in headlights
Smearing green signs and white lines
Only orange haze in darkness
And dips in Maryland roads

COUNTRY ROADS

Same strip of sky ambling and twisting
through the mountains but inverted.
Line of stars mirror the double yellow
coal trucks never follow,
I hear them rattle in my dreams.
Lumps of black, our diamonds;
they fall out over country routes
crushed to dust that coats Grandma's
kitchen window no matter how often
she scrubs it away.
She still swears by lime juice, though.
And I still drive this way,
over frost heaves and cracked pavement
where flash floods washed out the road.

From War to Caretta
three miles on route 16
then eighty through Bob White

and Bandytown to Twilight.
Dad lived in Van for awhile
and one Saturday I played
softball against Matewan
and had a grilled cheese
in the diner on Main Street
where a mom cooks and her
daughter serves. I'll bet
they had a Royal Crown Cola
sign lit up same as in 1920
when detectives from Baldwin-Felts
got into a gun fight with
my great-great uncle (I think)
at the depot near Chambers Hardware.
I'll look him up in the family tree.

FOG

Fog's so thick today
you can't even see across
the trains to trees.

My dream – don't crash the boat
on rocky shores!

MARA

Cat on window ledge
sniffs blinds and paws string.
Ears tick tock back and forth,
purrs, whirls to chase tail, falls.
They always land on four feet.
Meo-rrow.

HONSHU, WEST VIRGINIA?

Shift in basalt deep underwater,
so unlike shift in coal?

Not really.

Sandstone or slate atop,
time, and pressure.
Not Snyder's riprap
but dusted men and anchor bolts
under three-hundred foot thick rock.
Just take your core sample and
hope it doesn't flake.

DAY

Sunrise over pine needles
and your breath
quivers
in air above me.

SCAR ME

Some days I feel like Jackson Pollock.
I want to throw everything
out of my garage,
buy some canvas: drip dreams onto it,
smeared with a morbidity no one
ever understands.

Maybe I like the way blood mixes
with formaldehyde – forming
some watered-down orange that
could be finger-paint.

Eyes don't terrify me anymore –
            not yours or anyone's.
They're just layer on layer of cells
like everything else.

"Shouldn't it be a straight line?"

"Doesn't matter," he said, "no one cares
about their scars anymore."

It was too much.

I remember every scar I've ever seen
or touched. I fall in love with them.

They're like Pollock –
haphazard and chaotic,
but masters of beautiful.

And for just a minute I'm
in a dusty attic trembling
against the flat of a butterfly knife
chilling my skin.

COUNTRY

Crackle and spit
Thrum. Thrummmm.
Fire in its place, rain against the window.
No artificial light but
a single hearth against mysterious ink.
Tales waiting for a writer,
a place, a time.
And in the distance I imagine
horses whinny and maybe the clank
of bridle and bit.

NIGHT TRAIN

Horn blares in my dream.
The 11:30 train is early tonight,
warning.
GET OFF THE TRACKS.
Your smile is broken now,
honeyed wheat crushed by heavy rain.
Backpedal.
But if you have to go that's as
eloquent a way as any.
I'll see you across the tracks.

MOST ALIVE IN DREAMS

Familiar whorl of a fingerprint —
an entire relationship in micro-ridges.
Ice cracks in twenty directions
when dropped in my second Earl Gray.
Burns my tongue and
tastes like memory.

I kissed you in the bellies of
muscles and airplanes.
A little too sweet and soft
but it quenched my thirst.
Sangría without wine is just
fancy juice at its bones.

You write about gray as if
you've danced with it,
lived there for decades and
called it "friend".

I’m on a cliff, torn between
charcoal fingerprints and
brilliant scarlet —
a cape to retreat into when the
snow comes to bury us
and we forget to breathe.

GO BACK TO BED

Too early for birds —
it's February.
What happened to going
South for the winter?
Too early on Sunday —
pitch black outside but
I'm up and windows are open.
Hear the screeching, slowing
coal cars and — just barely —
see yellow markings.
Coal lumped inside,
black line stark against
blue-gray sky and mountains.
She slowly creaks back to life,
blowing in the distance, cars
clang into one another with
enough force to take your legs off
but the birds seem happy.

One thing for sure —
it ain't a Boston winter.

CRAYOLA

dark outside, my mood mirrors static pine
all knots and rough bark
two drops of black coffee spilled on floor
Mara licked them up before
I could find a towel
not sure if that's good for her or not
and hard to concentrate with
late sunrise — 7:36

a PSet would calm my nerves
but none of those now
only trigeminal vestibular
corticobulbar medial
longitudinal fasiculus for
company like it all makes sense anyways
when your notes are drawn in crayon
fitting since brains smell like a
box of 128 colors with a sharpener

CIPHER

The green isn't snapping anymore.
There are snowflakes
hanging from spikes,
lights intertwined and constant.
Soft, longing. I've missed it here.
Traffic, wind, and $12 dollar
movie tickets –
I think we'll still have to come back.
It's an addiction, the ever-present
Chapstick in my front right pocket.

And this time the SCIENCE
is of retrospection.
Memory. Psychic lobe and the limbic.
New words but it takes this room
to translate them and make them real.

BONE AND SKIN

Clavicles are sexy.
The way you lift one shoulder,
shrug, skin tightening as
line of bone says hello and
invites a kiss, or maybe two —
symmetrical, after all.

BLACK CELLOS

Dissonant cellos — off pitch and
simultaneous,like the warm-ups
I listened to with eyes closed
at Symphony Hall.
Every pitch passed under the
ever-watchful (at least) Beethoven.
I always thought Berlioz and Schubert
belonged up there too —
my three favorites presiding
over other greats:
Dvorak and his new world.
But no — these cellos belong to CSX,
and they're too close to my window.

FAR

Far from this world of
little shavings of eraser
you can't ever truly
            rub away
but
close to home — and heart — rise
Mountains of hard, black rock.
Up at 5 to see the
sun rise while
descending into earth.
Hard men drive Caterpillars
and Komatsus
in place of a grandfather's
pick and pail.
That pitch-black daytime thunders with
drills and dynamite;
fathers, brothers, sons even,
hacking.

His furrowed face meets furrowed tin,
coal-coated hands excavate those leftover
buttermilk biscuits his wife packed
in a washed white handkerchief.
Six days a week for the past
forty years.
Alarms blaze. Fireballs, like
dragon's breath,
roll, an underground
tsunami of white-hot ash and flame.
Rocks groan.
Sky of stone buckles, falls.
29.

For some:
A cold kiss on the
Forehead,
Spit, smudged with
Midnight dust.

www.ingramcontent.com/pod-product-compliance
Ingram Content Group UK Ltd.
Pitfield, Milton Keynes, MK11 3LW, UK
UKHW020216250726
13967UKWH00001B/27

9 781105 566530